UnMuted

Modern-Day Psalms to Liberate Your Soul from the Bondage of Stifling Silence

Sandra Valentine

ENDORSEMENTS

I have known my friend Sandra Valentine for many, many years. *UnMuted* reflects the contours of her heart as she grew and blossomed into the Woman of God that she is today. I commend *UnMuted* to you. If you enjoy poetry, like me, you are in for an important journey of reflection, identification and I may say freedom.

My favourite piece is "The Onion". It reflects the difficult work and cost of becoming real. The ancient wounds concealed with layers and layers of falsehood until the wrappings are peeled off and the "fragrance and flavour" fills the place and blesses others. Thank you Sandra for speaking into our sacred spaces from your sacred spaces.

- *Rev. Don Hamilton*

Truly inspirational. Innovative. Uniquely creative. *UnMuted* is no ordinary collection of poetry. You will undoubtedly join me in applauding this compassionate, very real guide to life-giving wholeness. A genuine understanding and interpretation of inner pain is evident throughout. You will relate to vivid illustrations that may reveal dismal, captive wounds crying out for release. Abundant direction will then illuminate the necessary expression of stagnant feelings buried far too long. You will, at last, be victorious, empowered by Christ's Hope!

- *Helen Browne*

DEDICATION

This book is dedicated to my spiritual father Pastor Alphonso Barnes who graduated to his heavenly reward on April 23, 2010. Thank you dad, for giving me a place, and the space to speak with freedom and experience freedom. Your genuine love and compassion *UnMuted* me.

ACKNOWLEDGMENTS

First and foremost I give honor to God for the privilege I have been given to be a conduit of His extravagant love, infinite mercy and unending grace. As a recipient of God's benevolence, I am constrained to dispense of what I have so freely received. There are many who have directly or indirectly participated in the process of seeing this work to fruition. I acknowledge my Professors at Palm Beach Atlantic University, Orlando campus... specifically Dr. Andrea Dyben and Dr. Montse Casado. Thank you for believing in me and inspiring me to turn my muse into craft. The members of Kingdom Life Center where I have been the senior pastor for over 19 years, you have been the potting soil where I have been given room to mushroom and grow. I am thankful for all of you who have faithfully shared and joyfully cheered. Your support over the years and specifically in this process have been the wind beneath my wings. I am also thankful for my friend Theresa Scott and for her obedience. The prophetic direction she shared ignited the flame and got me moving. Helen Browne, Don Hamilton, and Dr. Montse Casado, thank you for your endorsements of the book. Next, my three outstanding, heaven-sent friends, upon whose shoulders I have been able to stand tall, Helen Thomas, Marlene Greaves and George Scott. You are the best support anyone could ever ask for. Finally, to every person who gave me the honor and trusted me to see beneath your masks, I have carried your "stuff' as pearls in my heart. You have unknowingly freed me to 'Be'. I pray Psalm 20 over each of you and believe for a harvest to come to your life in super-size proportion.

CONTENTS

FOREWORD

I believe that within each of us lives a creative spirit—the artist within. People let this spirit come out in a variety of ways, from painting, to writing, to sculpting. For some - this spirit lies dormant throughout their lifetime. Either they believe it is not good enough or fear what may happen if they let this creative energy guide them. Creativity is like a seed, once you start watering it and feeding it, all it can do is blossom. That is exactly what Sandra has done in this book—she has allowed her spirit to have a voice, a message that will inspire others and bring much healing.

In my opinion, *UnMuted* gives voice to courage and faith. It is a dialogue with God and a reflection of one's inner world where all feelings are allowed. It provides an opportunity for the reader to connect with God in a different way. It is a dialogue that shares one's inner pain and desires. This book allows one to grow closer to God and become more of who one was designed to be. Enjoy the journey of creativity that is illustrated in this collection of poetry. And let the Muse inspire you and open your heart to your inner world. And with each poem, bring light to those dark places so the healing can begin.

-   *Dr. Montse Casado-Kehoe*

INTRODUCTION

U*nMuted* is a meditative collection of poetry designed to give voice to the human experiences of pain, shame, guilt, and betrayal - so familiar to us all, but which often have rendered us incapable of sharing, speaking, or expressing those deep internal struggles. It is my sincere hope that through this book you will access that place of suppression and be stirred to articulate your freedom with the aide of this written expression.

Personally I grew up in an environment where the allowance was not given to speak freely or even to own what I felt. Expressing myself freely, giving voice to my inner thoughts, fears, dislikes, or joy did not come naturally. It has been an evolution, emerging from years of feeling asphyxiated. Several factors contributed to the change in my life. Most importantly was my personal quest to be healthy—mentally and emotionally. The message of the cross is one of holiness as well as wholeness, and I wanted it all. Indeed, it was connecting relationally with others who were on a similar path that truly *"UnMuted"* me, and I came to understand quickly that if I was ever going to be healed, whole, and free it would never be in isolation but in the context of relationship. God designed it that way. It is not good to be alone. (See Genesis 2:18) Since I cannot know myself by myself, and I cannot heal myself by myself, by necessity I must connect correctly to emerge to the apex of my potential.

I remember the moment when the shackles finally broke. Through the process of healing, I now celebrate the marvelous freedom I have in Christ. I am FREE to FEEL—to cry, to hurt, to be angry, and to be expressive. I am FREE! And I believe that my freedom will enable someone else—perhaps you—to express inner thoughts and feelings. Often we hinder another's breakthrough because of our own imprisonment. You will be empowered as you read, reflect, or verbalize these poems. The particular ones that resonate deeply within you will unlock gates of captivity in your life.

These poems can be a therapeutic tool in your life, accessing the deep places in your heart. Just as playing or singing a song evokes certain emotions, may there be a similar response as God ministers to your heart. May you be *UnMuted*, even Unleashed. Break the silence and let your voice be heard! Muse upon what you hear. Don't run. You've done that long enough now.

Excavate! Reveal! Unveil! Remove the Mask!

LET YOUR HEALING BEGIN!

Many of the Psalms reveal raw and real emotions. Yet they always end in praise and celebration to the greatness and mercies of God. As you read, reflect and ponder that it was His grace and mercy that brought you through. It may have originated in the faulty parenting you received, the abortion you have never talked about, or the affair that destroyed your marriage. Perhaps it began with the incest that the perpetrator denied, the harsh condescending words spoken by a superior, or the lies that you were helpless to defend yourself against. You name it, for this list could never be exhaustive, since life is no fair game.

We've all been thrown to the curb at some point, leaving us with the question, "Why?" That's a question that can keep you stuck and imprisoned, for the answer may never come and even if it does, could never provide the remedy for your wounded soul. The decision must be made—personally and individually. Refuse to be labeled a victim for the rest of your life. Refuse to answer to the name that pain once called you. Arise when you hear the voice of the Master. Your hand may be withered, but if He says, "Stretch it out," then comply, knowing He gives both the command and the empowerment to fill the order. You may be crippled, but if He says, "Take up your bed and walk," then you can. You may be in a place where the maggots of life have eaten at your flesh and the garments of defeat are clinging to your soul, but when you hear Him calling your name, even from the grave, I say to you "ARISE!" No more excuses! No blaming, explaining, or justifying! If you do not admit it, you can never get rid of it. What you do not name will seek to bring you shame. What you do not reveal cannot be healed. James 5:16 (AMP) states, *"Confess to one another therefore your faults (your slips, your false steps, your offenses, your sins) and pray [also] for one another, that you may be healed and restored [to a spiritual tone of mind and heart]. The earnest (heartfelt, continued) prayer of a righteous man makes tremendous power available. Bring your past into the light of God's glory; in that place you will experience transforming grace."* Also see 2 Corinthians 3:18.

In His PRESENCE you will NEVER be ASHAMED. Just as Jesus did with the woman caught in adultery, He will stoop down to pick you up and He will say, *"Neither do I condemn thee: go and sin no more."* (See John 8:1-11)

This collection of poems has been set in three layers. The first is to remind you of God's awesome beauty and wonder. It is disheartening to gaze only on the depravity of this sinful age; here you have a call to ascend in your thoughts and gaze upon His glory. Even when His truth pierces you, it is only that He might heal you. See yourself in Him and He in you; it is a mystery but the Bible says that we are one with Christ. (See Colossians 1:27) The second layer is the premise for the book. Here you will find an expose´ of familiar internal struggles. This is the section I pray captivates your heart. As you read, I charge you not to touch that dial and not to silence the radar! It is your signal, your clue that something from the page resonates with something in you. What it is exactly, you may or may not be certain, but the Father is Faithful. He would never bring you to the mountain and demand your priceless "possession" if He had not already provided a ram. Abraham may never have seen the ram if he had not placed his treasure on the altar of sacrifice. (See Genesis 22:13) Your healing is wrapped up in you releasing your offering in the place the Father shows you. I am forever grateful for the day, the place, and the moment when I was granted grace to speak. Only God can orchestrate those moments and when we encounter them, we must seize them. Finally, you are invited in the third section of the book to ponder what is possible through the provision of the dynamic power of God at work in you.

This is your moment! Your time has come to break the code of silence! You have God's permission to speak! He is listening, and when you are ready, He will graciously appear with human ears through a confidant, a mentor, a pastor, a friend, or a counselor. You will disclose and then dispose of the excess baggage you have carried that has wearied you and kept you hiding from the crown. God chose Saul to be the king over Israel, yet when Samuel was ready to anoint him, He was hiding beneath the baggage! What is the baggage that is stalling your coronation ceremony? (See 1 Samuel 10:1; 17–22) You were born for a purpose, as is beautifully stated in Jeremiah 29:11: *"For I know the plans I have for you," says the* LORD. *"They are plans for good and not for disaster, to give you a future and a hope."(NLT)*

As you begin to speak, your heart will heal, yes, little by little. (See Deuteronomy 7:22) As your heart heals, you will connect with the untapped reservoir of grace that the world has been waiting for—your style, your beauty, and your creativity.

Creation happened because God spoke it into being—create your world with your words. Today be *UnMuted* **and let your voice be heard!**

PART 1

THE GLORY OF GOD

We were made in his likeness, created in His image to reflect the glory of God. I love and enjoy nature—speaking of which I am sitting in front of a lake a half mile from my house, writing. The sun is already perched on the balcony of the skies brilliant and glorious—a glory that is blinding to the eyes, should I dare try to gaze at it intently. The birds are up releasing their sounds—everywhere I look God's glory abounds—through nature.

  The creation speaks of the Creator—and so should we (see Romans 1:20). We are broken people. The residue of sin clings to our souls but even as the sun breaks through the dawn, so does the inner beauty of the divine yearn for release—not just in us but in all of creation (see Romans 8:22). The words of Albert Osborn's classical hymn express the same desire...

> *"Let the beauty of Jesus be seen in me,*
> *All His wonderful passion and purity.*
> *May His Spirit divine all my being refine.*
> *Let the beauty of Jesus be seen in me..."*

When we speak, we break the code of silence on our internal struggles. We open a gate that can lead others to gaze upon the light of God's manifested glory. The invitation has been given. Come go with me—behind the veil...

"And all of us, as with unveiled face, [because we] continued to behold [in the Word of God] as in a mirror the glory of the Lord, are constantly being transfigured into His very own image in ever increasing splendor and from one degree of glory to another; [for this comes] from the Lord [Who is] the Spirit."

- *2 Corinthians 3:18*

BEHIND THE VEIL

Behind the veil
No mask, no shame
Only authenticity
Just as I am, meeting with Divinity
My humanity, cascaded by His beauty
The place where I lose all consciousness
Of the sinfulness in me
Allowing His perfect grace to envelop me
No flesh, no works
Only surrender to the Power at work in me
Dressing me, shaping me
To reflect His radiant glory
A place of rapturous freedom and liberty
Basking splendidly in awe
Of who I am created to be.
Behind the veil
Lord, into me see.
No, not the ugliness I try to hide,
But the work of Christ completed,
finished in me.
Behind the veil,
remove all obscurity.
Cause me to see more clearly
the place I now occupy in the heavenlies,
Far above demonic powers and principalities
Behind the veil, emphatically
Oh! The rapturous beauty
of me in Christ and
Christ in Me.

GRACE

"The circumstances of our lives are pieces of a larger scheme in the puzzle of life, and in His Perfect Wisdom, the pieces fit."
- *Renae Jones*

Today, I pause to remember...
Grace for every moment of every day,
in summer or in winter,
You've shown the way.
You've kept me moving, inner-stirring.
Your word my feeding,
Your breath I'm breathing,
Your light is leading,
Your whispers I'm heeding.
The path is clearing the way You're making.
Today, I am leaning, resting on Your arms,
Sustaining, preserving, grace for advancing
to heights worth attaining
Destiny embracing, Your will obtaining
Now, there is no denying,
Grace is for the taking.

Reflections

Life is a cycle (sometimes you may even feel like you are in a circus) and at any given moment you may find yourself shuffling between the bleak chills of winter, the shedding and reframing of autumn, the brilliance and beauty of summer, or the sprouting of new shoots and the freshness of spring. Whatever the stage or phase, grace is available and applicable. Grace enables us to thrive, to conquer, and walk in victory. Consider the "season" you are in this moment, and reach for the empowerment of divine grace to help you stand and withstand the forces of adversity (see 2 Corinthians 9:14-15).

SHADES OF GLORY

Shades of glory is all I can see.
O the grandeur, the beauty, the majesty
His handiwork marvelously unveiled
In the expansive sky, the mighty sea
The ocean span, the land—then me
Inscriptions of splendor
In awe and wonder
I look and behold, He speaks to me.
The raging sea does not frighten me
For boundaries have been set by Thee.
The clashing of the ocean waves resoundingly
Echoes His supreme majesty
The darkened sky crowned with light
The galaxies command faith and sight.
O glorious beauty, wondrous splendor, all-consuming
majesty!
Though shades of glory capture me
It's but a call to bend the knee
To worship the King joyfully.

NATURE

Close to God
Discovering my divinity
Beholding His majesty
I see
Creativity
Magnificence
Intelligent Design
A call to worship
Sheer adoration.
My heart explodes with praise and song
To the One and only Great I AM!

Reflections

Read Psalm 150. The Psalm appeals for praise to be offered to God with everything and in every way. How do you praise God? What "instruments" do you use? Personally, I love to be in nature —particularly the ocean, which never ceases to evoke a song or poem from my grateful heart. List the place (s) that command worship from your heart...make a commitment to intentionally visit those places and experience your "face to face" with God. Jacob met God as he laid his head on a stone. (Genesis 28:11-17)

WORKMANSHIP

"Poeima"
"For we are the product of His hand, heaven's poetry etched on lives, created in the Anointed, Jesus, to accomplish the good works God arranged long ago."

- *Ephesians 2:10*

Some of the greatest sermons are never preached
For we think a big Bible and Pulpit we need.
The fact of the matter, art is the answer;
We are God's Poems.
He wants men to read them,
So start composing.
Yes, even the simplest lines of poems and rhymes
Are the most profound form of architectural design.
Yours may be the message conveyed through your art
That God will use to touch someone's heart.

Reflections

A recent graduation gift caused or I should say is causing a paradigm shift in my life — Emily Freeman in her book, "A Million Little Ways" has helped me to view whatever I do as 'Art' no matter how small or how great. On a sheet of paper list three things that you do very well. (Nothing is too small or too great.) Pick one and think of ways of how you can use that (your) 'Art' for His glory.

"Art is what happens when you dare to be who you really are."

- Emily P. Freeman

MOVEMENTS

"Your greatness is revealed not by the light that shines upon you but by the light that shines within you."

- *Ray Davis*

Movements created by You
Awesome power and presence vibrate
Reverberating the sound of Your voice
Silence every noise.
Produce, Reproduce
Your image in me
Let Your likeness be what others see.
Destroy every yoke!
Set me free from captivity.
Break the bands of the evil one
Liberate me by Your right hand
No Boundaries! No Limits!
I am bound for my Promise Land.

ROCKS

Stationary and strong, not built by man
Handiwork of God,
formed and forged by nature
Lightning and thunder, rain, snow, earthquake and sun
Hitting, splitting, ripping, settling, all forming.
The years it takes, the force embraced
Transforming to such polished beauty.
We fight and resist
Yet God persists.
We must display His beauty, His splendor.
Simply surrender!
The elements of adversity
Creating diversity, calling forth creativity,
To proclaim His majesty,
Rocks embedded in history.

Reflections

Read Philippians 2:13. Have you ever paused to ponder all the aggregated elements which have contributed to the person you are today? Everything you have been exposed to, everything you have experienced and every person you have encountered have influenced you in some way, either negatively or positively. Your response, interpretation, and reaction to these elements are what determine permanency of their effect. Nothing that does not have your cooperation and collaboration can control your life. How will you be formed? Will your life reflect the template that your circumstances have created? Or will the formation be the outworking of God's power and presence at work in you?

SPRING FORWARD

"There (is) order and even great beauty in what looks like total chaos. If we look closely enough at the randomness around us, patterns will start to emerge."

- *Aaron Sorkin*

Cycles, Circles, Rounds,
I am home base bound
From the beginning to the end
Supernatural grace abounds
Called Out
To Stand Out
To Show forth His glory.
There's no doubt, I carry His seed
His Story was born to be
Borne in me.

DAYBREAK

"Arise, shine; for thy light is come, and the glory of the Lord is risen upon thee."

-   Isaiah 60:1

It's the dawning of a new day
A fresh new morning
Crickets chirping, roosters crowing
A distant sound I cannot discern
The clouds clearing, the sun rising
From behind the shadows
Of rocks stationary and strong
Stately, even stunning, in their beauty
I behold the grandeur and the wonder
Instantly I join in the chorus
Of nature's creatures great and small
And with them proclaim,
"My God, How Great Thou Art!"

CALLED TO BE MORE

"Everything is appropriate in its own time. But though God has planted eternity in the hearts of men, even so, many cannot see the whole scope of God's work from beginning to end."
-     *Ecclesiastes 3:11 (TLB)*

Far beyond what I can possibly see
God has etched eternity inside of me
My finite mind can ne'er imagine
All that the Father has planned.
A future of faith
Fruitfulness and the fulfillment of prophecy.
Greatness lives inside of me
Today it screams, Set Me Free!
Let me outta here!
This place is too small for me!
The womb was for a season
but here is the reason
I cannot be contained
I am called to be MORE!
This is my destiny.

Reflections

"Now unto him that is able to do exceeding abundantly above all that we ask or think, according to the power that worketh in us."

-   Ephesians 3:20, 21

The Greek word for power is 'dunamis' — forceful, dynamic, ability, and strength is at work within you to produce and reproduce far more than you can conceive. So go ahead — yield, submit, surrender to the divine activity within.

PART 2

HUMAN PAIN

"I can help you accept and open yourself mostly by accepting and revealing myself."

                                    -   *John Powell*

How did sin get in? Who opened the gate? In Genesis 3 we have the account of the conversation that never should of happened. Adam and Eve entertained the propositions of the enemy and succumbed to the bait. The result—sin, hate, murder, anger, envy, strife and the list goes on. None of us escaped the impact of Adam's sin..."

"For I was guilty from the day I was born, a sinner from the time my mother became pregnant with me."

-   *Psalm 51:5 (The Voice)*

Sin is your design and mine; we do not need a class such as 'Sin 101' to learn how to sin; just being human makes us susceptible. The propensity and the proclivity to sin are inherent in our nature. No surprise, then, when the environment is conducive the seed breaks open and the "germs" begin to disseminate.

James 1:14 puts it this way, *"But every man is tempted, when he is drawn away of his own lust, and enticed."* I am attracted to sin because sin is in me...the sin in me produces pain, pain that is either self-inflicted or projected, so that your proximity may very well cause you to become infected and affected. Acknowledging human pain is to identify with the reality of the fallen nature of humanity. But there is hope...

Today another gate is open—the gate to God's presence, made possible through the provisions of Christ's atoning sacrifice. *"Enter into His gates..."* (Psalm 100:4). Access the antidote for sin, discover the place where you will be surrounded, secured and sustained as you navigate your way through the vicissitude of life.

LOVE WEEPS

"Love is never lost. If not reciprocated, it will flow back and soften and purify the heart."

- *Washington Irving*

Love weeps.
Whoever said that love will never hurt told a lie
I never knew but I found it to be true
Your heart aches, breaks, splits in two
For the love you gave, the vow you made, ends
abruptly.
Your life's disrupted, your emotions fragmented.
Your mind demented, memories cemented in your heart
lamented,
Sometimes tormented, looking for an answer
Who pulled the trigger?
Killing every dream you've lived for.
The truth is, the answer-love weeps
You cannot love and not get hurt
You won't ever give without realizing
That what you gave was priceless anyway
So why are you expecting someone to repay?
So keep right on loving
And never stop giving
You'll find that in living
With a heart that's forgiving
The pain is washed away.
For love sweeps.

Reflections

Tragic. The heart that is on 'lock down' —cold and frigid because of wounds that have become infected because of pain which has been neglected. (See Matthew 24:12) And how about you? Is there anything oozing from your soul? Have you become bitter and cynical because of betrayal, hurt, or disappointment? Let the Christ of Healing pour the antiseptic of His extravagant love in the wound...and if you weep let the tears flow, washing away every residue of dross, and pray that they will be medicine to your soul. Practice forgiveness and you will discover that the healing process accelerates the sooner you release and let it go...

"To forgive is to set a prisoner free and discover the prisoner was you."

- Unknown

IT

"He healeth the broken in heart, and bindeth up their wounds"
- *Psalm 147:3*
"If you do not tell the truth about yourself you cannot tell it about other people."

- *Virginia Woolf*

Where have you pushed "It"?
The abuse and encounter, rendezvous and experiment?
What shall you name "It"? Or can you?
Would that be to claim "It"?
The shame to admit "It".
You've said you'd never share "It,"
But how will you repair "It" if you don't name "It"?
"It" is generic, no label upon "It."
No one would ever hear "It"
You smile to disguise "It."
But the memories are there,
quite vivid and clear
So where have you placed "It?"
If only you'd dare to share
what you fight to hide
You'd find freedom and release with no more secrets to
keep
The message you "preach,"
your life would teach
Confession is for cleansing, the process of counseling is
for healing

Human Pain

The spirit is redeemed,
but the soul must be rebuilt,
The brokenness within does not negate
You've been cleansed from your sins.
I can hear the Father's whisper,
"The process never ends."
So to yourself be kind
I Am the Potter, you are the clay.
I'm shaping and molding you day by day.
The work I am doing is state-of-the-art
So I'm mindful while working not to neglect any part
Tugs and pulls, twists and turns, your heart does churn
For I am working my purpose for the world to view
My glory magnificently displayed in you.

Reflections

My testimony is censored and so is yours. No one tells it all and perhaps we could not even if we wanted to, sometimes wisdom necessitates the censorship. That being said, we should never be casual with our "pearls," (see Matthew 7:6) but we should be alert to grace moments divinely orchestrated, when we can be liberated from secrets that are debilitating, psychologically sociologically, physiologically and spiritually. I recommend that you read this verse from several different translations:

"When I kept things to myself [silent], I felt weak deep inside me [my bones wasted away]. I moaned [sighed] all day long."

-   Psalm 32:3 (EXB).

So while you may vehemently insist that your past is your past, and you may faithfully confess that your history is not your destiny...please take some time in quiet reflection and carefully examine whether there are patterns and cycles in your life that you cannot decipher...allow the light of God's presence to reveal anything concealed. Trust His grace to give guidance to the process and believe for the unveiling of a more authentic you.

"All that is left to bring you pain, are the memories. If you face those, you'll be free. You can't spend the rest of your life hiding from yourself; always afraid that your memories will incapacitate you, and they will if you continue to bury them."

-   J.D. Stroube

UNMASKED

"Never hide your fear because it will become your own God, hidden inside you."

- *Sorin Cerin*

"Me"
Masked, hiding, concealing
Afraid to reveal the truth
Untold secrets, hiding who I am.
I did not plan to stay in this place so long.
I thought I had only run for cover
Just to be safe 'til the storm was over
Never knew that pain could comfort me
It has become my new identity
Don't rip my mask
It is designed to protect me
Knowing even you might hurt me
I only trust me
Everyone else is a portrait of hypocrisy.
But the dark clouds of the night must give way
To the breaking of the morning's light.
Allow the Master to peel each layer
Carefully,
Precisely,
Skillfully.
The unmasked "Me" will discover a new identity.
"Me," endowed with gifts, talents and skills
The "Me" with no boundaries, no limits

Will climb and soar to the pinnacle of my destiny.
The empowered "Me" can now flap my wings, rising
above
Everything that tries to stifle "Me."
Even now my ears can hear the liberating, exhilarating
sound.

MARKS OF OFFENSE

*"A brother **offended** is harder to be won than a strong city: and their contentions are like the bars of a castle."*
- *Proverbs 18:19*

Many years ago your fire was hot,
you couldn't be stopped
You were running for the Lord,
filling every gap
Serving where you could,
ready and available;
You were on call, you were on demand.
Unaware that the enemy
had put a snare and a trap
A subtle plan to have you offended by man.
Sure you did not see it coming
You'd never leave your soul unguarded
And in the moment you weren't looking
He charged into your heart,
Bit like a viper
Snapped like a revolver,
Bashed by a hammer.
Before you knew it the damage was over
Your spirit was wounded by words not intended
And actions, yes, you were offended.
At first you denied it
"Not me you chided, I'm too big for that derailment."
Yet the signs were so glaring

UnMuted

You tightened your circle
Complained to whoever would listen.
Justifying and defending your pain and your
positioning.
Neutralizing His voice,
Ignoring His Word.
You were offended and you wanted to be heard.
Offense is a killer
Its ultimate goal is to remove you from your place
he's after your calling and purpose in God.
Remember he has fallen and aims to get us all
To miss the mark, the prize of our high calling in God
So get up my friend
Shake off the cloak of offense
Forgive and be mended.
Refuse to be lost over such a trivial cost
For the sake of the cross take off the mask.
Let Christ heal your scars
Remove the defense get rid of offense
Then your soul can breathe once again.

Reflections

Selah! —*Pause, ponder, and meditate on this. Before you move on, listen to your heart that has been stifled, even suffocating under the weight of this covert sin. Bring it out of the dark and into the light. Then your soul can be liberated and you will be rid of this blight! Forgiveness is the only response that will free your soul from this entrapment. No, it is not the dismissal of your pain; it is the discarding of the chains. You may never hear the words "I am sorry, please forgive me..." This is a decision predicated on your obedience to God. If you can, confront the situation head on, get it out in the open...what you drag into the light loses its strength — elicit the wisdom of a mature, neutral voice, and work through the pain. The process may take time, but be patient, set healthy boundaries, and determine the new way you will now engage. Prayer is cathartic and therapeutic. Pray for your offender; at first it may be awkward and seemingly disingenuous but keep going. Eventually, one day you will awake to the realization that your heart no longer aches. Now you can file the experience as part of your history.*

- *Matthew 6:12 (AMP)*

HEAR MY CRY

"To understand people, I must try to hear what they are __not__ saying, what they perhaps will never be able to say."

- *John Powell*

Don't see my anger
Feel my pain
It's only a mask
It's only a game
I've played it so long
I am ashamed to even call it by name
For so long I've fought
To keep people off
With tentacles of wrath
Only to be left with more scars on my heart.
The very thing that I need is what I repel.
Not knowing that in opening my heart it would heal.
So if you can move beyond my flagrant display
I know you'll discover a heart that's been broken,
needing to recover
Hoping you'd love me unconditionally
Hoping you never judge me
When my brokenness you see.

Reflections

Anger is another word for pain. I was enlightened in my recent studies in Counseling Psychology to the fact that anger is a secondary emotion. Often it is a mask for pain. Do you know someone that you have quarantined from your life because of an anger problem? Or are you isolated because others have become afraid of your tentacles of wrath? The next time you see the display, ask the question either of yourself or of another, "What is hurting you?" Be mindful however, that the answer may be unknown or the question may seem absurd. In either case let the awareness be an alarm. I caution you, not to hit the snooze button. Throw off the covers...now that you have been awakened, appropriate the medicine, ask God to heal, open the wound to the Great Physician and let the antiseptic of His Word, the oil of His presence and the care and compassion of His body—the Christian community—restore and heal you.

"A void in my chest was beginning to fill with anger. Quiet, defeated anger that guaranteed me the right to my hurt that believed no one could possibly understand that hurt."

- *Rachel Sontag*

THE ONION

"Our deepest wounds surround our greatest gifts."

- *Ken Page*

Layers wrapping each wound
Secretly constructed deep within my soul;
Dark, ugly, hatred brews
The truth conceals, the fake revealed
No one will know I'm not healed
It's time for the onion to peel
Layer by layer the stories of pain
All for another's restorative gain.
Though you may cry for a while
Your fragrance and flavor released
Will assuredly benefit another.

Reflections

I dislike peeling onions. I have not met anyone who does. What I like though is the flavor it gives to my cooking. The process is irksome — inevitable tears will flow from the burning sensation in my eyes. This reminds me of my own life. I am a composite of many layers, and the deeper the work the more tears will flow. Nonetheless, consider the satisfaction of the taste, the flavor, and the smell as you eat the meal—that is the goal that must be kept in view. Beloved, your life carries an aroma that the world desperately needs. Though the process of peeling is painful to say the least, resign yourself to the process, for only then will the deposit you came to the earth to release be fully expressed.

"But we have this treasure in earthen vessels, that the excellency of the power may be of God, and not of us."

-    2 Corinthians 4:7

ALONE WITH MY THOUGHTS

"Only the truth of who you are, if realized, will set you free."
                                        - *Eckhart Tolle*

All in your head
Swish swash
The volume is so loud
You're sure others can hear the sounds.
The thoughts of painful memories haunt
The things you regret
Desires unmet,
Fears of countless stories untold
You fight to maintain control.
Bring to the surface of your mind
Those things in excavating you find
Do not suppress, it will de-press.
Let your thoughts be sequestered
Into the hands of the Masterful Conductor
He'll arrange the notes
Synchronized and harmonized
A Beautiful Orchestra.
Alone with your thoughts, run to your Lord
Your cry for healing He won't deny.
Memories revealed
In His presence will heal.

Reflections

I have made an observation, perhaps you have too. Busyness is a form of avoidance. Stay busy and I do not have to deal with my issues. Solitude is a forgotten spiritual discipline; we tend to leave that for the monks in some isolated monastery. It may seem a contradiction to mention in a book that is encouraging you to break the code of silence to be told you need to foster silence in your life. The difference is one form of silence stifles; the other takes you beyond superficiality...the place and space where you face the truth of who you are and why you are. So carve out some time to sit and be alone. See what surfaces. Invite grace balanced with truth to sit with you and trust the Father to walk with you through the length of the journey. Be attentive that His appearance may be veiled with human face.

"I can only know that much of myself which I have the courage to confide in you."

- *John Powell*

ISOLATION

(SATAN'S SUBTLE PLAN)

"One may have a blazing hearth in one's soul, and yet no one ever comes to sit by it."

- *Vincent Van Gogh*

The enemy wants to isolate you
Telling you no one understands
No one can truly empathize and feel your pain.
He is counting on you lashing back
Countering the perceived attacks
With thoughts that hold you back
From fellowship that can close every gap.
The lies from hell you must repel—the truth of God
upheld.
More are with you than are against you
So mind your head, guard your heart against every
demonic onslaught
Remember the victory obtained through the power of
the cross.

Reflections

"We were born in relationship, we are wounded in relationship and we can be healed in relationship. Indeed, we cannot be fully healed outside of a relationship"

-   Harville Hendrix

Got it? That is the divine design. (See Genesis 2:18) Aloneness often breeds loneliness although one can be alone but not lonely. The application is to reflect on what perhaps is more dangerous to your emotional and mental well-being. Isolation is a place of disconnect and detachment; it is a place where "fire-walls" are erected, supposedly to protect you but in actuality they separate you from the sense of belonging, that you need from other human beings. One of the lessons we can learn from the animal kingdom is that seldom do they travel alone; they travel in groups where it is safe, secure, and supportive. Who do you have surrounding you? In whom can you confide? Who can locate and identify with a great degree of accuracy where you are on the emotional, mental, and spiritual radar? Ask God to connect you correctly. In Ezekiel's Vision of the Dry Bones, (See Ezekiel 37) the bones kept moving until each was fitted perfectly. Somewhere out there in the vast universe are some 'perfect fits' for you, though the fits may not be perfect. Pray and believe that the wind of God's Spirit will create a movement and unite you to and with those who are part of your destiny.

"The person who tries to live alone will not succeed as a human being. His heart withers if it does not answer another heart. His mind shrinks away if he hears only the echoes of his own thoughts and finds no other inspiration."

-   Pearl S. Buck

JEALOUSY

"...Jealousy is cruel as the grave."
- *Songs of Solomon 8:6*

Have you ever looked at someone's blessing and asked
yourself
"How come, you, and not me?"
Did you recognize that awful sting?
Jealousy, yes name and shame it!
Don't let it hide in obscurity
Amputate it!
Before it spreads throughout your being
Leaving you lame
My friend, it's no game
It's ugly and as cruel as the grave
It will make you plan and devise a scheme
To destroy another man
It will turn into hate if you don't annihilate
Hear this warning again
Jealousy is not an innocuous thing.

Reflections

Okay so who has never felt jealousy steaming within? How can you identify the spirit of jealousy? How do you react when someone other than yourself is promoted, blessed, recognized, successful, gets married, or has children? Perhaps it is more about watching someone's "basket" getting filled while yours remains empty. For Joseph (See Genesis 37:4; 11) it was his gift of dreaming and interpreting dreams, and it was the coat bequeathed by his father that stirred hatred in his brothers. I believe jealousy is the seed of hatred of which murder is the fruit. The death is not always physical. If you recognize jealousy in your heart swiftly confront it. It can cause spiritual death, snuffing the life of the Spirit of God out of you, and it causes relational death. You will grow cold in love towards the one you are jealous of. Deny habituation in the sanctuary of your soul, sever ties, serve the eviction notice today, do not delay, and rid your soul of what will erode and ultimately manifest itself grotesquely.

BETRAYAL

"Only those you trust can betray you..."
- *Terry Goodkind*

Believe behavior
Ignoring signs – No! You weren't blind
This flaw you weren't seeking to find
The sacred trust given
was treated with dishonor
To be given such a privilege
Like Samson and Delilah
You gave hint to your strength
Never expecting it would become revenge.
Now your heart is sinking with an awful feeling
Intoxicated with confusion
Staggering with no comprehension
But the behavior is true
Your perspective is skewed
Try as you may, you'd never understand
Except to contend
Many are the flaws of mortal man
So turn to the Word
God's truth will shed light
The way made bright
As you journey through the night
His glory your soul will console.

Betrayal (ON TRIAL)

"Sometimes the person you'd take a bullet for is the person behind the trigger."

- *Taylor Swift*

Betrayal always leaves clues
Signs and signals, meta-messages
So many things done all meant to charm
Yes for sure they'd say, "It won't harm."
Flattery to get you
Stories all a lie
No denial, when put on trial
Schemes and gimmicks they were in it to win it.
How could they hide; they weren't on your side?
This was a 'self-help' game
A game that left you in pain
The consequences they couldn't see
Blurred vision
Causing division.
Arise! Court is in session
Here comes the judge
Examine the evidence
To this there would never be an objection
That betrayal is guilty causing undue cardiac strain.
Now render a verdict on the behalf of the plaintiff
Then send a stern message so others would refrain.

Reflections

Jesus and Judas: the Biblical narrative that provides the best frame-work from which to glean what betrayal looks like. Betrayal is possible because of proximity; only someone close can betray you, thus the intensity of the pain...'WWJD' (What Would Jesus Do). So what did Jesus do? He sat with his betrayer, served his betrayer, and "surrendered" to his betrayer. He chose his response and maintained and managed the results. So how are you managing that aspect of your life? Are you in control or are you being controlled by the ugliness of bitterness and rage? Take consolation; Jesus knows how it feels to experience the cold kiss of betrayal. Take your heart to the altar, let it be consumed by God's holy fire, make Him your sole desire, and your passion He will re-fire.

DISTRACTIONS

"Just because something isn't a lie does not mean that it isn't deceptive. A liar knows that he is a liar, but one who speaks mere portions of truth in order to deceive is a craftsman of destruction."
- Criss Jami

The plan ensued
The gestures proved
My heart was won
Worn like a medallion
Assured you are the one.
Access granted, the choice was made
Into my sacred space you came
Little by little my walls came down
Before I knew it, 'twas all on the ground.
What was my desperation?
Why no hesitation?
The words were lavished
For this care I was famished.
The game was one sided
I warned and I chided
You can hurt me indelibly
But you responded sublimely
You are the only one for me.
The signs are now glaring
You've walked out without caring
For the treasure you were given.
The dark side of me ignored all the signs
The extravagant love made me blind
But God by design uncovered my eyes.

Reflections

Just because it is good does not mean it is good for you. Can you discern when the "good" thing is preventing you from experiencing the best thing— a life overflowing in the presence of God? What is worth you selling out? Money? Sex? Power? Promotion? Material Possession?

"For what shall it profit a man, if he shall gain the whole world, and lose his own soul."

- Mark 8:36

Warning signs that you are distracted; this thing or person draws you away from God, not to God. You compromise your values, you distance yourself from the people who love you, and you show contempt for the things you once enjoyed. If any of these symptoms exist in your life stop what you are doing and call the emergency hot-line to heaven, race to the "ER," and ask for admittance into the Intensive Care Unit. Do not delay. Regain your focus, recalibrate, and get back on track.

DON'T DO IT

"If I expose my nakedness as a person to you, do not make me feel ashamed."

- *John Powell*

In each of us there is a measure of fear and insecurity.
Why then do we play upon the chords of another man's vulnerability?
Perhaps I'm unaware of my own depravity
Seeking unconsciously to bring you on par with me
Unknowingly, reflecting back to you
The fear lurking inside of me.
And if my time is spent examining you
There'll be no time to look at me
Be careful then, exercise caution
If another man's "treasure" you've been given
It's very rare you'd ever see
The **authentic, inner me.**
So if I dare to step outside,
Away from the cover of my pride
Please be gracious should I confide
Those things for so long hidden.
Let's make the choice to cover each other
Never exposing
Causing more pain, collaborating, to perpetuate shame.

Reflections

To judge another is to assume you have all the data. Such an assumption is rather presumptuous since only God is omniscient. As recipients of grace we ought to allow our lives to be conduits of this marvelous virtue that is so vital for the sustaining of the human soul.

"...Freely ye have received, freely give."

- Matthew 10:8

Take a moment to confess to God where you are guilty of judging another. Accept His love and grace (the Holy Spirit has just given me a check—we often judge others because we ourselves are ridden with guilt and condemnation over past or present sins. Wow!) Meditate on Psalm 103:8-10. The same principle is applicable here; if you do not forgive yourself you are making yourself more righteous than God. Really? More righteous than God?

"...All our righteousness are as filthy rags (menstrual cloths)"

- Isaiah 64:6

Not admissible as evidence to adjudicate. In Christ alone can we be absolved from our sins. (See 1 John 1:9) Cleansing comes through confession. Simple, do it and it is done!

RE-ARRANGED

Color codes, themes and throws
In every corner, in every room
My furniture's set.
Then, life entered
like a whirlwind
S-h-i-f-t-e-d
Re-arranging Everything

FEAR

I can only know that much of myself which I have the courage to confide in you."

-   *John Powell*

Fear incarcerates
Seeks to dominate
Perpetuates lies.
Distorting the view
Sabotaging relationships
Aborting dreams
Causing vision and
mission to end in futility.

Reflections

The assurance that I am fully loved and completely accepted dismisses fear from my life. Think of how you can build bridges of love in your relationships so that the chasm of fear can no longer divide hearts that are meant to unite?

*"There is no fear in love; but **perfect** love casteth out fear: because fear hath torment. He that feareth is not made **perfect** in love."*

- *1 John 4:18*

THE BOOK

Your life is a storybook with many chapters inside
Each tells its own tale
of glorious triumphs and places where you have failed.
Pages, should you rip them?
Evidence and matters you are tempted to hide.
But, before you discard them,
Remember, they're a part of you.
Your pearls, your treasure
Don't casually display them.
Some chapters are for **'Reference Only'**
You see, this is your library and you can decide
Who is worthy of reading the contents inside.
So discern very carefully
Don't cast your pearls before "swine"
You are the author and your book, copyrighted.

PART 3

REDEMPTION & HEALING

"Owning our story can be hard but not nearly as difficult as spending our lives running from it. Embracing our vulnerabilities is risky but not nearly as dangerous as giving up on love and belonging and joy—the experiences that make us the most vulnerable. Only when we are brave enough to explore the darkness will we discover the infinite power of our light."

- Brené Brown

The prefix Re- means to do again. Christ came to earth to re-deem man, to buy back what His Father originally owned, and to restore what was stolen by the enemy.

"He came to seek and to save that which was lost..."

- *(Matthew 18:11)*

Imagine the travesty if there was no hope of healing, deliverance and redemption from our depravity? God is omniscient—He knows all things and so He pre-destined you before the foundations of the earth. He determined the boundaries of your life (see Psalm 16). He has determined the exact places where we should live (see Acts 17:26). God saw the collision before it happened—your repair has been pre-paid and prepared, tailored with specifications, and all in the master's plan. Adam and Eve tried to use fig leaves to fix their problem—temporary masks will not suffice; this time open the gate of your heart and invite the Savior in (see Psalm 30:2).

"God can heal your broken heart but you must give him all the pieces"

- *Unknown*

THE DARK ROOM

The place where I will take your negative
And develop a beautiful portrait of you
So don't be afraid of the darkness
The place of acquiescence
Is a place of formation
The cocoon is only for a season
Soon it will be a butterfly
So my beloved know that you are a treasure
Yet to be discovered
Your true worth no man can measure.

DEEPEN THE FOCUS

"Listen to God with a broken heart. He is not only the doctor who mends it, but also the Father who wipes away the tears."

- *Criss Jami*

Lord, in this place of deep contrition,
Please, hear my petition
Remove every partition
Let there be no division
My heart united- integrated
Lord make me whole.
In this place grant relief,
So be it if my heart feels grief.
I'll let the tears flow
Lord, I'm letting go
So you can mend my brokenness
For this heart could never heal
If from You the broken pieces are concealed.

MEASUREMENTS

"You get one pass at life. That's all. Only one. And the lasting measure of that life is Jesus Christ."

- *John Piper*

Don't measure your worth by the systems of man
Name brand clothes, luxury car and plush mansion
Don't measure your success on how much you've achieved
Be ever mindful of whom you are seeking to please,
Don't sell your soul and end up in hell.
It's not how many times you fell
But how many times you got up again
It's not the breath, but the depth of our times together
These are things that really matter
It's not the price or the size of the gift
But the fact that you did remember.
You see I measure your care not by the things you give,
But the deep thoughtfulness, and the rich treasure to my life you bring.

- *Read: Matthew 6:25-34*

STILL WE RISE

*"We are hedged in (pressed) on every side [troubled and oppressed in every way], but not cramped or crushed; we suffer embarrassments and are **perplexed** and unable to find a way out, but not driven to despair."*

-    *2 Corinthians 4:8 (AMP)*

Still We Rise
Though torn and beaten
Still we rise
Though stripped and forgotten
Still we rise.
The Master's pleading
His voice we're heeding
We know He's leading
For still we rise.

THANK YOU

"Gratitude makes sense of our past, brings peace for today and creates a vision for tomorrow."

- *Melody Beattie*

Thank You Lord
For grace to press beyond the problem.
Thank You Lord
For Love to move beyond the betrayal.
Thank You Lord
For the peace in the midst of every trial.

Reflections

"Consider it a sheer gift, friends, when tests and challenges come at you from all sides. You know that under pressure, your faith-life is forced into the open and shows its true colors. So don't try to get out of anything prematurely. Let it do its work so you become mature and well-developed, not deficient in any way."

- *James 1:2-4 (AMP)*

"In everything give thanks...."

- *1 Thessalonians 5:18*

"Your attitude determines your altitude"

- *Zig Ziglar.*

So you choose — to grumble or be grateful, be bitter or be better, to be pitiful or powerful. Choose this day to be thankful, you will discover your "tank" is full with more reasons to praise than to pout.

Cultivate the attitude of gratitude...start a gratitude journal; at the end of each day write five things you are thankful for, for that day. Rehearse your blessings and erase your grumblings. Start today and make everyday a 'Thanksgiving Day.'

"Count your blessings, name them one by one, count your blessings see what God has done, count your blessings, name them one by one and it will surprise you what the Lord has done."

- *Johnson Oatman, Jr., pub.1897*

HE LEADS THE WAY

"A ship is safe in harbor, but that's not what ships are for."
- *William G.T. Shedd*

The blackened night obscures my sight
There's a command to break camp
Valiant soldier advance!
Arise with thy might.
There is a call to fulfill
The Master's purpose and His will.
You will never discover the conqueror within
If in the harbor you remain safely anchored
Launch out into the deep
Trust Him your soul to keep
Light beams from heaven
Illuminating the eyes,
Floods of visions
Crystallizing your aim
Divine guidance
Guaranteed to sustain.

"O send out thy light and thy truth: let them lead me; let them bring me unto thy holy hill, and to thy tabernacles."
- *Psalm 43:3*
Take the first step in faith. You don't have to see the whole staircase, just take the first step."
- *Dr. Martin Luther King Jr.*

LORD REFRESH US!

So repent (change your mind and purpose); turn around and return [to God], that your sins may be erased (blotted out, wiped clean), that times of refreshing (of recovering from the effects of heat, of reviving with fresh air) may come from the presence of the Lord.

- *Acts 3:19 (AMP)*

Times of refreshing Lord,
For this we pray
Send down your rain upon us today
Wash every stain of sin away.
With your love and grace open the floodgates.
Pour out upon us the Holy Ghost's fresh fire
Ignite us with holy passion
We want you to be our only devotion.
Rend the heavens now come upon us,
Let the earth receive heaven's sound
May our hearts reverberate with prayers that re-sound
Like the mighty noise from the upper room.
We pray for a "Church-quake" let everything shake
'Til people awake to the call from Your throne
To fill the whole earth,
Your glory released everywhere.

Reflections

*Do you long for revival—is there a deep yearning within to experience the manifest presence of God? Great! You are at the starting point—revival begins with desire, fueled by the spiritual disciplines of confession, prayer, and fasting to name a few. It is all or nothing, total abandonment to God of every dream, desire and aspiration. When He becomes our everything we lack nothing. We live in a materialistic age. We want God's **presents** more than His **presence**; we desire His **hand** more than we do His **heart**. Continue the journey, and turn your longing into pursuit. He has promised that those who seek Him will find Him (see Jeremiah 29:13).*

FEELINGS...

"To tell you my thoughts is to locate myself in a category. To tell you about my feelings is to tell you about me."

— *John Powell*

Awaken emotions...
Feelings, desires...
Dreams, fears...
Longings, yearnings...
Owning
They're all a part of me.
Drowned beneath the noise of my past
Saying that's all history
Barring, blocking, barricading...
Preventing me
From clearly seeing the path to be free
Free to soar
Creating, remaking...
Evolving,
Releasing His Divinity
Release! Release! Release!
Untie me, loosen my hand, my feet
Run! My heart throbbing, hair raised,
Nose burning, brow sweating
Feelings, but, yes, I'm letting go
No longer anesthetized
I am fully alive
The emergence of a butterfly

UnMuted

Awakened to my destiny
I'm aligned with Divinity
I am after His kind
To call forth and create
The orchestra now plays
Rushing, healing sounds
Abound from heaven's gate.

Reflections

Feelings…can you trust them? Do they have a role in how you live your life? Or are they like squatters illegally occupying your "land"? I recommend that you begin paying attention to your feelings as they emerge, erupt, or just linger. They are signs and signals that you should not ignore. When you feel a pain (especially if it is persistent) in your body you want to know what is the cause. Likewise, conduct an inquiry when you feel something: Is God alerting you to something? Is the light amber, red, or green? Should you stop and listen, exercise caution before you proceed, or can you take the leap? Is there some unfinished business and "account" that needs to be closed? Be attentive to the signals sent from your emotions. Do NOT be led by them but rather wrestle with what you are feeling and why; in this you will discover answers that you may not receive any other place.

HUSH... HEAR THE FATHER

*"...In returning [to Me] and resting [in Me] you shall be saved; in **quietness** and in [trusting] confidence shall be your strength..."*

- *Isaiah 30:15 (AMP)*

The voices, the noises, the clamor the chatter,
They mutter, they stutter
Devouring my ability to be still.
The rest of the Sabbath
Must bring to a halt
All the movements and actions
distracting my heart.
Solitude and silence
Lord, help me be still
Give me the ability
To discern Your divine will
Your voice I will follow
When I hear Your whisper
"This way," says the Master.
Today I hear You calling my name
I'll run with abandon
Away from the pain
I've discerned hell's assignment
To pull me into its net
Constantly muttering,
"Your life's a mess!"

"Not so," says the Master.
"Your cry has been heard
To know Me much better
For this you have yearned.
My child, take my hand
You'll never walk alone."
"For today," says the Father,
"Your heart is my home."

CHOOSE LIGHT

Two roads before you lay
Choices you must make today.
Which road will you take?
Go to the Light
Don't stumble in the dark
Make your decision from an enlightened heart
Each day you decide in whose will you'll abide
The pressure of the voices can lead you astray
There is peace in following His will
Exuberant joy in submitting to Him
Though uncertainty drapes the path
Choose the light
Follow God's heart.

I'M NOT AFRAID

Isaiah 43:1-2
"What lies behind us and what lies before us are tiny matters
compared to what lies within us."

- *Ralph Waldo Emerson*

Out of the boat my feet upon the ocean deep
The Master has called me
Oh! My feet are slipping
I think I'm sinking
But I'm not afraid of the wind and waves.
Snarling, roaring voices of giants all around
Trying to scare me,
With their intimidating sound
I will not run and I will not hide
For God's presence in me abides.
His gentle voice whispers ever so clear
"My child, do not fear
Though storms appear
Know that I am near."

SURRENDER

"Only God is capable of telling us what our rights and needs are. You have to surrender that right to Him."

- *Joni Eareckson Tada*

I give myself away
Relinquishing every right
I give up the fight
Secured in His Might
I walk to the light
Even through the night.

LIGHT YOUR WORLD

"And you, beloved, are the light of the world.
A city built on a hilltop cannot be hidden."
- *Matthew 5:14 (VOICE)*

Flashlight pointing in the wrong direction
Fellow Christians pay attention
Shine where there's darkness
It's the world than needs our attention.

DESTINY CALLS

Destiny calls, I'm forsaking all
To follow His plan and obey His commands
Though adversity befalls, I'll carry the cross
For sweet victory awaits me at the end of it all.

In Him I Am Free

"A healed memory is not a deleted memory. Instead, forgiving what we cannot forget creates a new way to remember."
- *Louis B. Smedes*

Thank you Father...
For saving me
Keeping me
Delivering me
Setting my face, fixed towards destiny.
Thank you for destroying the evil sinister plans of the enemy
In You I have the victory.
Thank you for eyes to see way beyond my history
My past no longer has a hold on me
Through you my God I am completely free.
Satan said it would never be
Those grave clothes would still hang on me
And though you are out of the fire
The smell of smoke on your clothes will never expire
But God has transformed me
I am not the man I used to be
Weak, frail and full of timidity.
The enemy no longer has a hold on me
I am full of divine clarity
The path He's made for me
I'll walk with my head held high
In truth and dignity

UnMuted

His love and power bought my purity
The stains are gone
From pain I am free
The Christ of Calvary—He's my victory!

WORK OUT

"There is no exercise better for the heart than reaching down and lifting people up."

\- *John Holmes*

Body movements...
We are ***s-t-r-e-t-c-h-i-n-g***
Flexing our muscles, feel the tension
Exercise those joints
Get rid of the stiffness
Oxygenate the body, remove all impurity
The whole flowing with ease and precision
Synergize, so we will accomplish the goal
Bringing God's Kingdom from heaven to earth.
What we do not use, we will lose
So let us build Christ's body with stamina and power.

Reflections

I have recently developed a new hobby—Classical Stretching—a form of exercise that strengthens and flexes the entire body without high impact. Paul uses the metaphor of the body to describe the church - Christ's body. Consider how relating and engaging in a Christian community requires you to stretch in your thinking and behaving. Many times the discomfort can be felt in the joints and the muscles; they go on alert perceiving danger just like we have the tendency to do when called to engage in authentic fellowship. The goal is to keep flexing, and let the tense muscle know it is okay to relax. This will not hurt you; it will strengthen you. In my counseling training, I learned a valuable lesson regarding resistance—we resist for a reason, so rather than fighting the resistance you flow with the resistance. The body, spiritual and natural, must learn to move harmoniously to create synergy (see Ephesians 4:15-16; 25).

SYNERGY

"The whole is greater than the sum of its parts."

—   *Aristole*

Father,
Let this be our desire
To be yoked as true bond-fellows
In purpose united
For destiny joined.
Paired for the journey
Look what we've accomplished
When our rights we relinquished
To be part of the convergence
Flowing together
Achieving the ultimate
Through synergy.

BREAK THE JAR

"It is possible to give without loving, but it is impossible to love without giving."

- *Richard Braunstein*

We give with caution
We ration the portion
Clueless it seems, to Whom our honor is due.
He spared no expense when He died on the tree
Giving His life for you and me.
Offer your life as a burnt offering
Withholding nothing - break the jar!
So should you struggle to regain
There'd be naught to reclaim.
Whatever you deem your costly treasure
Like David of old, let us be bold
Offering nothing of a cheapened sort
Nothing bleak, nothing weak
Not insipid, nor apathetic.
With a life full of passion
Pursue His presence.
Release the fragrance from above
Your life adorned with the aroma of His love.
Touching, Healing, Delivering
Transcending Grace.

INNER LONGINGS

"We need never shout across the spaces to an absent God. He is nearer than our own soul, closer than our most secret thoughts"
- *A.W. Tozer*

Insatiable desire
Innate
Carved by God
For Him we crave.
Hide and seek
He conceals Himself
Obscured by the darkness.
Darkness and light are the same to Him
This message to us was written
To our hearts it was given.
So then, it is the manner of our eyes
Trained by the circumstances of life,
Sight fragmented
Reading faultily.
Lord, give us Your eyes, that we might see more clearly
Take us higher
Provide a panoramic view
Help us go deeper, diligently seeking
Ultimately knowing
That it is for You we're longing.
Satisfy us with good things
Bring absolute contentment
You are enough

Hear our prayer, consume us
And may our hearts forever cry-More.

*"And the Lord shall guide thee continually, and satisfy thy soul
in drought, and make fat thy bones: and thou shalt be like a
watered garden, and like a spring of water, whose waters fail
not."*

- *Isaiah 58:11*

CRACKED POTS

*"But we have this treasure in **earthen** vessels, that the excellency of the power may be of God, and not of us."*
- *2 Corinthians 4:7*

The vessels were made in His likeness and beauty
Fulfilling their purpose and destiny
Created by the Potter's design
Each with its uniqueness, proud of its rarity
Never seeking notoriety.
Exposed to the elements
These little beauties began chipping
First the outer layer peeling
Then before long another coating
Revealing the scars
Where once beauty lay.
A closer look reveals it's in the Master's hand
That all this chipping and peeling began.
He is after the core
The external is mere shell.
Before we judge another by the outer coat
We should call this to remembrance
The valuable vessel, although cracked
Attests to the truth,
Bears witness of the fact that
God still uses cracked pots.

"God uses broken things. It takes broken soil to produce a crop, broken clouds to give rain, broken grain to give bread, broken bread to give strength. It is the broken alabaster box that gives forth perfume..."

- *Vance Havner*

STEP OUT OF THE BOAT

"I learned that courage was not the absence of fear, but the triumph over it. The brave man is not he who does not feel afraid, but he who conquers that fear."

- *Nelson Mandela*

I hear the voice of the Master calling
But another voice within me—contending,
"You won't be sustained."
Who has ever seen-
Water congealed a platform to walk upon?
Reason and logic opponents of faith
Echoes the waves intimidating sound
The hand of the Savior
My support, my anchor
Faith ignited
Fear retreats
As I plant my feet upon the ocean deep
I lift my gaze to see the eyes of love embracing me
His grace drawing me
Reminding me that by His power
I can walk upon the sea.

Reflections

God seems to place orders too tall for us to fill. Right? Peter and his risky faith...all he needed was to hear, "It is I." Can you discern who has called you to a task bigger than you? Do you believe that the provision will equal the vision? Then step out of the boat. No, leap! Only those who would dare leave the place of comfort and familiarity will experience the sense of triumph and accomplishment.

"But without faith it is impossible to please him: for he that cometh to God must believe that he is, and that he is a rewarder of them that diligently seek him."

-    *Hebrews 11:6*

IMAGINE C-H-A-N-G-E

"Never compare your journey with someone else's. Your journey is your journey not a competition."
- *Cheryl Jacobs Nicolai*

Who would have thought this could ever be
A creepy crawling caterpillar
Transformed into rare beauty
A butterfly with wings, not tentacles that sting
From darkness and obscurity
God brings to light its destiny.
For years it seems,
You, too, have wiggled and turned
In a place you've said, "I think this is home."
No hope in sight, "If this is my plight
I might as well accept, why fight?"
You have watched while others passed you by
Seems like you would never win
Faltered here, stumbled there
Surely you've had your share of pain.
But what you didn't know, what you couldn't view
Were the goals and plans He had for you.
I have learned it took years, you see,
For an oak tree to stand strong and sturdily
Nothing great evolves in haste
The Sistine Chapel took years to paint,
The patriarch Noah built an ark
With steady gaze and persistency.

UnMuted

Some things take time to develop and grow
So they can serve the Master's will.
My Child as I look at you,
The magnificent work of an Architect I see
What at first looked like cluttered mess
Now revealed, portrays the Father's Best.

*"Not everything that is faced can be changed, but nothing can
be changed until it is faced."*

- *James Baldwin*

Epilogue

The following poem is the impetus for the fulfillment of the dream to write and publish revelatory thoughts and ideas that have forever been etched in my head. I shared this poem as part of my Multicultural class presentation in Greece in June 2013. After the class my professor, Dr. Andrea Dyben, declared these words to me, "You have quite a talent there and you should do something with it." Little did I know that exactly one year later, I would be directed to publish a book of poetry that would break the code of silence on internal struggles and pain.

Pain does not discriminate and is not limited to any gender or color. Every breathing human being knows the cold kiss of betrayal, the heartless thief called death, and the snarling voice of fear. The voices of many have been silenced by trauma and their survival kit is just to "stuff it" and simply hope it will go away. When was the last time you gave expression to your true feelings? Or are you scared of being so real? You fear others won't know what to do if your true colors come 'shining' through. There goes the enemy's lie!

The truth is this: your true colors would paint your world with authenticity.

DON'T JUDGE ME

Don't judge me from where you stand, saying
"Oh No! She is a woman"
You've read the text, yes, all out of context
To substantiate your pretext in attempt to refute my
prefix
Yes, I am a woman.
The Call of God upon my life is the only reason for this
parody
I am not a feminist, I am undeniably feminine.
I am not usurping authority, I have been endowed with
authority.
I am not an afterthought, I am God's forethought.
I am not doing this because a man resists
I am doing this because God insists.
I know you throw scriptures around
Saying, "I am out of my league"
but read again before you proceed.
Wasn't Deborah a judge, a ruler in Israel?
Esther, as God's choice,
not just a queen, but a deliverer indeed.
Oh! and Phoebe, Junia, Priscilla, Tryphena and
Tryphosa,
Women all, who heeded The Call.
But listen my friend, please listen well,
When you tell me to be silent, ignoring the cultural
context

Remember, Jesus was born not of ordinary human
descent.
Read His genealogy in the first chapter of Matthew
again.
Abraham begat Isaac, Isaac begat Jacob,
Jacob the twelve tribes of Israel...
A closer look at verse 16 will reveal,
It was through Mary, a woman, that God brought forth
His Seed,
So, if God who is all-wise, chose not to disguise
That a woman is worthy to bring forth His Son,
Would He not release a woman to speak forth His
Word?
When tempted to judge,
Request an "In Camera," a moment with The Judge.
Raise an objection and ask God if you must,
"How could You, being so wise and omniscient, put
your anointing upon a woman?"
Now render your verdict
Upon the evidence presented
Lay aside your prejudice
It is time for admission
That the gift of the woman
Plays an integral part
In fulfilling the GREAT Co-Mission.

I wrote the following poem on January 22, 2014, the third year anniversary of the accident that catapult me into my destiny. Psalm 91 is one of my favorite passages of the Bible. The experience made this Psalm more personal and real. I am grateful that I am alive to tell the story.

If in some way your life seems like you have been through a 'Train Wreck' and the impact of life has left you fragmented inside, know this: God is in the business of redemption. He will pull you from the wreckage. He will restore and make you whole. You need only to listen to His voice. Run to Him, not from Him. Abandon the "vehicle" that has carried you all through life. While you may lose that familiar, even 'treasured' mode of performing, today a new day is dawning.

TRAIN WRECK

Sitting in my car—traffic was tight
It was on an ominous Saturday night
I was tired and drained from the warfare I was in,
The plan I now know was to distract and oppress—the
enemy's goal was to annihilate me
But angels, poised to obey the Master's command were
on duty
On January 22, 2011 at approximately 7:45p.m. '**The
Dispatcher'** from heaven said,
"You must go now! To the railroad crossing on
Poinciana Boulevard,
My daughter is in trouble, but this tragedy is **NOT** to be,
She's yet to complete her Destiny
To the left, the train lights were all I could see,
Too late now, the railroad gate was coming down on me,
With no place to go, I heard a whisper say— **"Get Out"**
Motorists were blowing their horns, frantically,
They were trying, hoping to "awaken" me
But it was an angel you see, that pulled me from the
impending tragedy.
It's all a blur but, this I recall
In slow motion I opened my car door,
and then I ran from the car about 200 feet,
In seconds my car was hit, sending parts all over the
street,
The sound of the collision sent shivers throughout my
entire being

100

UnMuted

I wanted to be held by anyone after what I had just seen
Still in shock, I ran to a lady and begged for a hug,
But she too seemed to be in a fog
Then God sent His earthly angels, Apostles Sam and
Myrna Malave,
They were on their way to an event but oh, they came to
comfort me.
I hugged their necks and broke out in tongues.
Today, with a grateful heart I still sing His praise—Yes,
with a new song.
It is three years since this surreal experience,
I celebrate with joy the third year of my "New
Beginning"
For this one thing I know, the enemy cannot kill me,
God has me folded, wrapped in the Center of His Will,
No plot of hell and no scheme of man can ever thwart
the Father's Plan.
My Destiny is fixed and I will not Exit the earth 'til I've
done ALL He has asked,
And then, I will hear my Father say, **"Welcome my
child; Well Done, Well Done!"**

Dear Reader:

Thank for purchasing my first book, or perhaps it was a gift. Either way, I believe that God orchestrated the connection. I have prayed for you, and I am praying for you. Nothing is a coincidence. I believe *UnMuted* is part of the divine plan of God to bring you into healing in a fuller more meaningful way. You have been called before the foundation of the earth to be a Carrier and a Courier of the Kingdom of God. To do so you must have more, so you can give more, experience more so you can communicate more. We cannot give what we do not possess; we cannot possess what we have not experienced. God's plan is that you would stay on the path.

Commit to the process of living with your soul liberated from the bondage of stifling silence. Keep talking. As you continue the journey of living a life *UnMuted*, I ask that you would take the time to share with me how *UnMuted* has helped you. Your feedback will be welcomed. Drop me a line at the email address below, and connect with me on Facebook.

Shalom!

Sandra

Website: sandravalentineministries.com

Email: unmuted@sandravalentineministries.com

Facebook: facebook.com/SandraValentineMinistries